Th Cateran Trail

a circular walk in
the heart of Scotland

Jacquetta Megarry

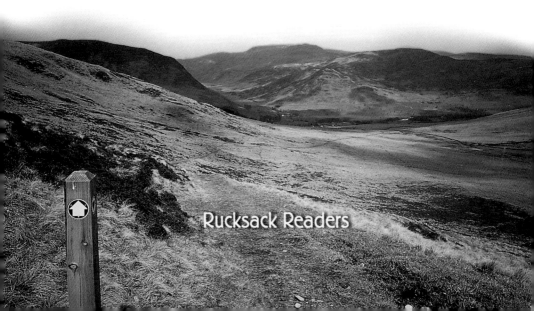

Rucksack Readers

The Cateran Trail: a circular walk in the heart of Scotland

First edition published in 2004 by Rucksack Readers, Landrick Lodge, Dunblane, FK15 0HY, UK

Telephone   +44/0 1786 824 696
Website   **www.rucsacs.com**
Email   info@rucsacs.com

Distributed in North America by Interlink Publishing, 46 Crosby Street, Northampton, Mass., 01060, USA (www.interlinkbooks.com)

ISBN 1-898481-21-0

British Library cataloguing in publication data: a catalogue record for this book is available from the British Library.

Designed by Workhorse Productions (info@workhorse.co.uk)
Colour separation by HK Scanner Arts International Ltd in Hong Kong
Printed in China by Hong Kong Graphics & Printing Ltd

The maps were created for this book by The Linx of Edinburgh, based on Ordnance Survey mapping by permission of the Controller of Her Majesty's Stationery Office © Crown Copyright, Licence no 100039026.

Publisher's note

All information has been checked carefully prior to publication. However, individuals are responsible for their own welfare and safety, and the publisher cannot accept responsibility for any ill-health or injury, however caused.

The Cateran Trail: contents

Foreword

Laurence Blair Oliphant of Ardblair and Gask, Chieftain of the Blairgowrie and Rattray Highland Games

As a local landowner whose family has ancient roots in Perthshire's history, I am very pleased to have been asked to pen a foreword to this book. The caterans, after whom the Trail is named, were a particularly bloody and ruthless crew of vagabonds who used the route regularly, and often for ill purpose. It is to the credit of the Perth and Kinross Countryside Trust that these infamous local outlaws are now being made famous. In opening up a new Trail, a pathway into Scottish history has simultaneously been forged.

My own family, I hasten to add, were not known to be caterans. Based at the family seat of Ardblair Castle, we were, and remain, staunch Perthshire Jacobites. We are part of a farming family that has been working with the land for over six hundred years. We welcome visitors from all over the world onto our farm in Blairgowrie for the Highland Games, held annually on the first Sunday of September. We regularly recreate historical battles at this event, and we enjoy sharing our rich past with interested parties. I believe there to be no finer place on earth than Scotland, and I fully understand the impulse to explore her history and her territories.

Co-operation between landowners and walkers has made this venture possible. I wholeheartedly welcome the responsible visitor to the area, and hope to support the initiative fully. Your courtesy and consideration is not only appreciated, it is vital to the avoidance of tensions between walker, farmer and landowner. Let us enjoy the Trail in the way this book suggests (see page 10), and leave behind any conflict in the past, with the caterans.

1 Planning to walk the Trail

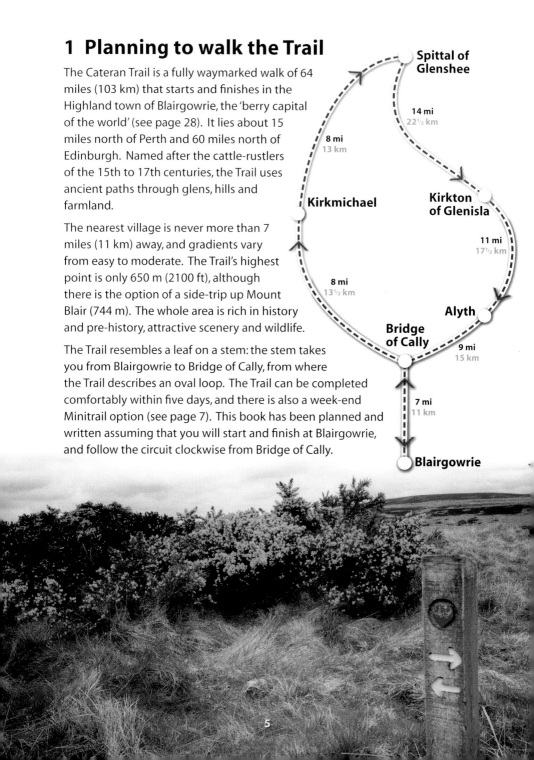

The Cateran Trail is a fully waymarked walk of 64 miles (103 km) that starts and finishes in the Highland town of Blairgowrie, the 'berry capital of the world' (see page 28). It lies about 15 miles north of Perth and 60 miles north of Edinburgh. Named after the cattle-rustlers of the 15th to 17th centuries, the Trail uses ancient paths through glens, hills and farmland.

The nearest village is never more than 7 miles (11 km) away, and gradients vary from easy to moderate. The Trail's highest point is only 650 m (2100 ft), although there is the option of a side-trip up Mount Blair (744 m). The whole area is rich in history and pre-history, attractive scenery and wildlife.

The Trail resembles a leaf on a stem: the stem takes you from Blairgowrie to Bridge of Cally, from where the Trail describes an oval loop. The Trail can be completed comfortably within five days, and there is also a week-end Minitrail option (see page 7). This book has been planned and written assuming that you will start and finish at Blairgowrie, and follow the circuit clockwise from Bridge of Cally.

Spittal of Glenshee

14 mi
22½ km

8 mi
13 km

Kirkmichael

Kirkton of Glenisla

11 mi
17½ km

8 mi
13½ km

Alyth

Bridge of Cally

9 mi
15 km

7 mi
11 km

Blairgowrie

If you decide to walk the Trail anti-clockwise instead, you will have to reverse the book's sequence and directions.

Most of the walking is straightforward, along tracks, paths and forest or minor roads. Some of it is boggy underfoot, or involves stream crossings, or is exposed and must be taken seriously, especially in doubtful conditions. If this is your first long-distance walk, read page 11. Before doing the Trail, most people will benefit from some long day walks, to test their feet, gear and general fitness.

No long-distance walk in Scotland should be undertaken casually, because the weather is so unpredictable. On any given day, you may experience weather typical of any season, and perhaps of all four. This adds variety to the experience, but also underlines the importance of being well-equipped and well-prepared.

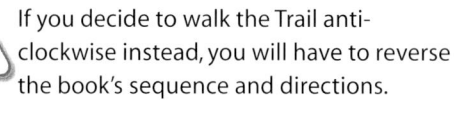

The Trail has many stiles, some tall

How long will it take?

To complete the Trail comfortably, allow five days. Table 1 shows the daily distances, and Part 3 describes the Way in five sections, each corresponding with one day's walking. If you have only four days to spare, you could limit yourself to the circular loop, omitting Blairgowrie. You can begin and end this walk at any point, such as Alyth, Bridge of Cally or Spittal of Glenshee. Please park considerately if arriving by car.

Table 1 *Daily distances for a 5-day walk*		
	miles	km
Blairgowrie	15	24$\frac{1}{2}$
Kirkmichael	8	13
Spittal	14	22$\frac{1}{2}$
Kirkton	11	17$\frac{1}{2}$
Alyth	16	26
Blairgowrie		
Total	64	103$\frac{1}{2}$

Each night you will reach a village where there is a choice of refreshments and accommodation, although you are advised to book well in advance. Specialist providers can organise it all for you, or you can book for yourself using the list provided by the Tourist Information Centre or websites (see page 62).

For those who wish to camp, there are campsites at Blairgowrie, Bridge of Cally, Ballintuim and Alyth (see page 62). Wild camping is not allowed anywhere on the Trail without the landowner's permission.

The Cateran Minitrail variation lets you sample the Trail's fine scenery within the space of a week-end. On day one, walk the Trail from Kirkmichael to Spittal. On day two, follow the Trail as far as Cray, leaving it to head westward to Kirkmichael via Lair (total distance 20 miles/32 km, see page 52). You could spend an extra night at Spittal, perhaps to take in some serious hill-walking (see page 20).

You can walk the Minitrail anti-clockwise instead, or start it at Spittal instead of Kirkmichael. But if arriving by car, do not start from Lair or Cray, since neither has any suitable parking.

Table 2 *Distances and shortest journey times between selected places*

	miles	km	by bus	by train	by car
Perth/Blairgowrie	15	24	45m		30m
Edinburgh/Perth	45	72	1h 30m	1h 15m	1h
Glasgow/Perth	62	100	1h 40m	58m	1h 15m
London/Edinburgh	400	650	9h 30m	4h 20m	7h 30m

Planning your travel

To plan your travel, consult the maps together with Table 2, which shows approximate times for reaching Blairgowrie by various methods. Bus and train times are the shortest as scheduled in 2004. Car journey times are based on driving within speed limits, making no allowance for traffic hold-ups, and with minimal fuel stops. If you arrive in Scotland by plane, you could rent a car at the airport and arrange to leave it with one of your accommodation hosts, at your own risk.

All figures are rough guidelines only: contact details for transport providers are given on page 62. Check timetables carefully in advance, as not all services are daily, and in winter the services tend to be less frequent.

The circular nature of the walk makes car travel a convenient choice for visitors who wish to combine hiking the Trail with other activities, such as sightseeing, golf, fishing or genealogy. Nowhere on the Trail is more than 40 minutes by road from Blairgowrie, which may be comforting to know, in the event of an emergency.

Grassy mound in summer (the Tomb: see page 39). Inset: Above Enochdhu in winter

What is the best time of year?

Fortunately for those who have little choice over their holiday dates, any season can be suitable. Be prepared for cold, wet and windy weather at any time and you may be pleasantly surprised. Here are some factors to ponder:

- Winter is far from ideal, because the days are so short: at this latitude daylight lasts for only 6-7 hours in late December.
- On winter timetables, public transport is less frequent.
- In summer, hikers may suffer from pests such as midges (tiny biting insects) and clegs (blood-sucking horse-flies).
- In summer, there will be more pressure on accommodation; however, many B&Bs close for the winter.

On balance, and if you are free to choose, the ideal months are probably May/ June and September/early October.

Navigation, waymarkers and safety

The Trail is fully waymarked, sometimes with modern posts, elsewhere with older, more rustic signs (as shown on page 5). Look out for these, especially at junctions, and try to remember the most recent waymarker, as well as looking for the next one. If you haven't seen a waymarker for 20 minutes you are almost certainly off the Trail. Retrace your steps to the last waymarker, check your map and compass and try again. Despite the generally clear waymarking, some walkers get lost, perhaps because they are distracted, or perhaps because a waymarker has been covered by vegetation, or damaged by an animal or vehicle.

For the Trail itself, you might rely wholly on the dropdown map in this book, together with the waymarkers and a compass. However, to follow any of the related walks in Part 4, you need to carry a compass and the relevant map (see page 63), and know how to use them. The walks in Part 4 are not generally waymarked, and to follow them safely you need some navigational competence.

There are possible dangers from road traffic, where the Trail crosses a busy main road, or follows one very briefly. In the longer sections of minor or single-track road, walkers must be alert for motor vehicles, including motor-bikes. Normally if there is no pavement, it is safer to walk on the right side of the road, so as to face oncoming traffic. However, depending on sight lines and the location of any verge, it may sometimes be safer to use the left side. Remember that drivers may not be expecting to see walkers: help them by wearing bright colours, especially in poor visibility.

Do not rely on a mobile phone for personal safety: reception may be poor or your battery may be low. It is unfair to disturb wildlife and other walkers with mobile chatter, so if you must carry one, please be considerate about using it. There are public phones in the villages, pubs and in many accommodations.

In the outdoors, the person ultimately responsible for your safety is yourself.

Landowners and responsible walking

Most of the Trail lies on farmland and pasture, and its route depends on the goodwill of some 30 landowners. Perth and Kinross Countryside Trust has negotiated written agreements with these individuals over the years, so as to allow the Trail to be routed across their private land, with suitable waymarking, stiles and gates. A single thoughtless walker can jeopardise goodwill that has taken a long time to develop. Common sense and courtesy are, as always, a walker's best friends.

The countryside may be your playground, but remember that it provides a livelihood for its residents. Lambing takes place mainly between March and May/June. Never disturb pregnant ewes, nor approach young lambs, or their mothers may neglect or abandon them.

If you meet cattle on an unfenced section, give them a wide berth: they may resent your presence. Although an attack is very unlikely, take special care not to go anywhere near a cow with calf, and stay alert until you are well clear of the hazard.

Deer stalking and game shooting take place near the Trail at various times of year. Felling is a vital part of forest management. Such activities contribute to the economy of the area. Please keep to the waymarked route and observe local signs.

The Scottish legal framework on access rights and responsibilities is changing just as this book goes to press. Traditional restrictions may be called into question with the approval of the *Scottish Outdoor Access Code* (see page 61). Meanwhile, please follow the Country Code.

> ### The Country Code
>
> ✓ **Respect the life and work of the countryside.**
>
> ✓ **Guard against all risk of fire.**
>
> ✓ **Leave gates as you find them, open or carefully closed.**
>
> ✓ **Keep dogs under strict control.**
>
> ✓ **Keep to established footpaths, to reduce damage.**
>
> ✓ **Use gates and stiles to cross fences and walls.**
>
> ✓ **Leave livestock, crops and machinery alone.**
>
> ✓ **Take litter home.**
>
> ✓ **Help to safeguard water supplies.**
>
> ✓ **Protect wildlife, plants and trees.**
>
> ✓ **Take care on country roads.**
>
> ✓ **Avoid making unnecessary noise.**

Dogs

Dogs – even well-behaved ones on leads – are not welcome on the Cateran Trail. Visiting dogs do not mix well with resident livestock, and responsible dog-owners will understand the importance of respecting landowners' wishes. If you have dog withdrawal symptoms during your walk, the advice is to stay at the Spittal of Glenshee Hotel, where the manager maintains a splendid tradition of lending his well-trained resident spaniels to any guests who wish to take them for walks.

Never approach a young lamb

What to bring

People vary widely, both in what they need for comfort, and what weight they can comfortably carry while they walk. If you want to bring more than the bare minimum, you may want help with baggage handling. Consider booking accommodation through a provider who can arrange baggage transfer for you (see page 62). Otherwise you could organise it through a local taxi firm.

If you book accommodation independently, start by reviewing what you need to walk comfortably each day. If the overnight extras are little more than clean underwear and a toothbrush, consider carrying them too, rather than relying on baggage handling.

Look through the packing checklist on pages 12-13 before deciding your approach, and plan any important shopping well in advance. Once on the Trail, shops are few and choice is limited. On many sections, there are no refreshment opportunities en route, so you must carry everything you need for the day.

New to long-distance walking?

If you've never tackled a long-distance walk before, welcome to a healthy and engrossing type of holiday. With sensible preparation, a healthy person of any age can complete the Cateran Trail. You don't need to spend a fortune on special gear, but suitable, well-tested walking boots are essential.

For advice on choosing gear (such as boots, rucksack, gaiters, poles, water carrier and blister treatment), please obtain our *Notes for novices* (see page 63). Try out some day-long walks before committing yourself to the full distance. If you are new to long-distance walking, do not attempt the Trail alone, especially in winter.

It's a common mistake to underestimate the time you need. Walking steadily on the flat, you may average about $2^1/_2$ miles per hour (4 kph) overall. If the route is uphill, or the ground boggy, or there are frequent obstacles such as stiles and streams, expect 2 mph (3 kph) or even less. (These figures allow for brief pauses to admire the view or take a photo, but exclude longer stops, e.g. for meals.) On this basis, the 8 miles from Kirkmichael to Spittal may take 3 to 4 hours, whereas the 14 miles from Kirkton of Glenisla to Alyth might take 5 to 7 hours of walking. However, the worse the conditions and the longer the walk, the more likely you are to need rest stops. Allow greater margins for longer days.

Packing checklist

The checklist below refers to your daytime needs, and is divided into *essential* and *desirable*. Experienced walkers may disagree about what belongs under each category, but novices may appreciate a starting-point. Normally you will be wearing the first two items and carrying the rest in your rucksack.

Essential

- comfortable and waterproof walking boots
- suitable clothing, including specialist walking socks
- hat (to protect against cold and/or sun), gloves and waterproofs
- water carrier and plenty of water (or purification tablets)
- food or snacks (depending on distance from next supply point)
- guidebook, map and compass
- blister treatment and first aid kit
- insect repellent: expect pests in summer months, especially in still weather
- toilet tissue (biodegradable)
- waterproof rucksack cover or liner, e.g. bin (garbage) bag
- enough cash in pounds sterling for the week

Cash is suggested because credit cards are not always acceptable and cash machines are very scarce along the Trail. Bin bags have many uses, e.g. storing wet clothing, preventing hypothermia (cut holes for your head and arms).

Desirable

- whistle and torch: these are essential if you are doing any 'serious' side-trips or hiking in winter
- pole(s)
- gaiters to keep mud and water out of boots and off trouser legs
- binoculars: useful for navigation and spotting wildlife
- camera (ideally light and rugged): remember spare batteries and film/storage
- pouch or secure pockets: to keep small items handy but safe
- weather (sun and wind) protection for eyes and skin
- spare socks: changing socks at lunchtime can relieve damp feet
- spare shoes (e.g. trainers), spare bootlaces
- notebook and pen.

(If you are camping, you will need much more gear, including tent, groundsheet, sleeping mat, sleeping bag, camping stove, cooking utensils and food.)

Kilometres and miles, metres and feet

In this book, distances are given mainly in miles but heights mainly in metres, in line with the hybrid system that has crept into modern Britain: road signs (and Trail signposts) show distances in miles, whilst on maps, contours, spot heights and grids are in metres and kilometres. The diagrams below may help you to convert between systems. Here are some easy rules-of-thumb:

- metres and yards are roughly interchangeable, at least in this book in directions such as '150 metres after this junction ...'. To convert metres into yards more accurately, add 10%.
- to convert feet to metres, divide by 3 (and round down by 10%)
- to convert miles to km, add 50% and round up a bit.

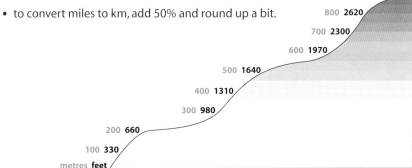

2·1 Caterans and cattle

Highland cattle used to be black, long-horned and long-haired (like this modern animal), but smaller

The word *cateran* comes from the Gaelic *ceathairne*, meaning 'peasantry'. It came to mean the fighting men of a Highland clan, especially those who stole cattle, and also irregular soldiers and marauders generally. Parts of the Trail follow ancient routes along which these hardy cattle were driven.

Cattle were highly valued for their milk, meat and hide. Having enough beasts could make the vital difference to whether a family could survive the winter. Cattle were a form of currency, and cattle-rustling a popular type of theft.

Caterans were active from the late 14th to mid-17th centuries. A group might consist of 50 to 500 men, drawn from various clans, but with a chieftain elected to lead the raid. They would descend from the high ground, moving at great speed over rough terrain to plunder the farmland below. Covering up to 50 miles in a single day, they took advantage of surprise by attacking at night.

The raids were violent, the caterans attacking many scattered smallholdings at once and killing the menfolk. The women might be handled roughly, but not seriously hurt, and children were never harmed.

Strathardle was a natural gathering-point for the glens nearby, and a market was established at Sillerburn, Kirkmichael. Sillerburn ('silver burn') took its name from the custom of sealing a bargain by handing silver coins across flowing water. Cattle bought there would be taken south to Dunkeld or south-east over Cochrage Muir (the high ground near Bridge of Cally) to Blairgowrie.

In about 1390 Duncan Stewart, an illegitimate grandson of King Robert II, led a raid to the rich farmland of Angus. This led to a running battle, as the caterans were pursued into Strathardle, the fighting beginning at Glasclune near Blairgowrie. The Angus men, who included Sir Walter Ogilvy, Sheriff of Angus, Sir David Lindsay of Glenesk and a number of armoured knights, were beaten off.

The Angus force regrouped to await reinforcements, and later caught up with the raiders. Bloody fighting followed, and the Angus men were again heavily defeated, with Sir Walter Ogilvy amongst those killed. The site became known as Dalnagairn ('field of the cairns') after the custom of raising cairns to the dead, both as monuments and to stop wolves and foxes from digging up the graves.

The fierce fighting of the Highlanders is shown by an incident from this battle quoted by historians and by Sir Walter Scott. Sir David Lindsay had speared a cateran, pinning him to the earth, but the dying man still managed to swing his sword and cut Lindsay to the bone through stirrup and steel boot.

Caterans continued to raid these glens for centuries. John Grant, or *Cam Ruadh* ('one-eyed redhead') was a renowned archer of the early 17th century. He devised a plan to defeat and deter the caterans by adding a lame white cow to a herd of the black cattle as a secret target. The white cow was just about discernible, even on the darkest of nights. When the herd was run off by caterans, the white cow hobbled along, trying to keep up. Cam Ruadh took aim behind her pale shape, and picked off several raiders.

The rest of the caterans then panicked, but Cam Ruadh guessed their route and ambushed them near the Kindrogan bridge at Enochdhu. It is said that the stones of the burn were stained red with their blood, and the place is supposed to be haunted to this day. The Strathardle Archers still have a field archery course 'meticulously designed to retain the natural feel of a simulated hunt' nearby, about one good bowshot from this very spot.

Kindrogan Bridge, where the caterans were ambushed

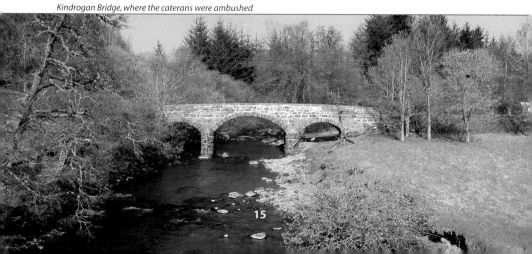

The Spittal of Glenshee Hotel, formerly the Spittal Inn

One of the last raids recorded in the area was also the largest ever in scale. In 1602, a band of 500 caterans attacked simultaneously in Glen Shee, Glen Isla, Strathardle and three other glens, rounding up more than 2700 head of cattle which had been spread over a huge area. They mustered the cattle at the Spittal Inn, and were planning to drive them north through the Cairnwell Pass.

Near the top of the pass known today as the Devil's Elbow, the local clansmen began their counter-attack, at first with only 150 men but increasing in strength as men arrived from other glens. The battle was savage and chaotic. Its turning-point was the arrival of Cam Ruadh leading the Gleann Taitneach men. His archery was so deadly accurate that he alone was credited with killing 40 men.

The raiders were almost surrounded, and half of their number dead, including their leader. The survivors were so desperate to escape that they cut the throats of the cattle, relying on this to delay their owners who would try to save the valuable animals. Many raiders and some cattle escaped, and the price the locals paid for defending their property was terrible. Nearly 400 men were killed, many households having lost all their menfolk as well as some of their cattle.

The era of cattle-rustling was ended by the gradual spread of law and order from lowlands to highlands, reinforced by the availability of firearms.

2·2 Farming since the Middle Ages

The valleys of the Cateran Trail have been inhabited since pre-historic times. The many ancient standing stones, cup-marked rocks and burial mounds marked on maps are evidence of this. Although the area has been farmed for some 5000 years, many of the visible remains date from the improving agriculture of the 16th to 19th centuries. This section focuses on features that a walker can easily see, on or near the Trail.

Strathardle and its kilns

In medieval times, much of the strath (valley) of the Ardle was owned by the Church. The land was highly valued for its rich grazing, well-wooded slopes and water-powered mills. You will pass several disused mills on the banks of the Ericht, on your first day's walk through Blairgowrie.

From the Trail, the most obvious agricultural feature of Strathardle is its lime-kilns: the one in the photograph below can be seen from the Trail near Kirkmichael, see page 33. The lime was needed to counteract the acidity of land reclaimed by drainage of peat-bog and swamp. Following the spread of roads in the 18th century, seams of limestone between Kirkmichael and Dalrulzion were dug up and used as the raw material for lime fertiliser.

Many kilns were created throughout the area, especially in Strathardle. Kilns were generally built into a hillside. The limestone was packed in layers, alternating with charcoal, which was then fired. Once the carbon dioxide was driven off, the sponge-like stones would be removed and left to break down in the rain, before being spread on the fields to improve crop yield.

A lime-kiln near Kirkmichael

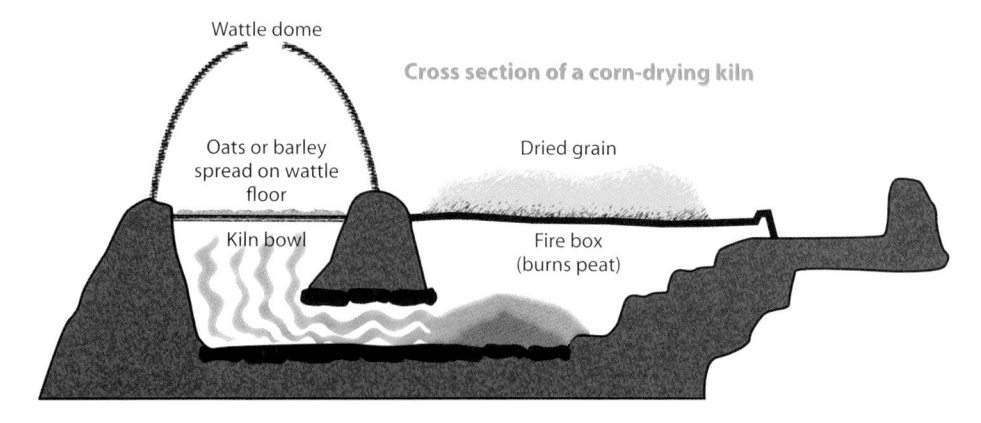

Cross section of a corn-drying kiln

Wattle dome

Oats or barley spread on wattle floor

Dried grain

Kiln bowl

Fire box (burns peat)

By contrast with lime-kilns, very few corn-kilns survive, although there is a rare example to the east of Kirkmichael, see the photograph below and directions on page 54. Their function was to dry sheaves of oats and barley before threshing and grinding, and they were common throughout the Highlands from medieval times. The Scottish climate meant that drying was essential before grain could be processed, eventually to become flour and other edible products.

Above the kiln bowl were wooden joists to support the drying floor of wattle (interwoven thin, flexible branches). These were woven closely enough to prevent the grain from falling through, while still allowing warm air to pass upwards from the bottom of the bowl. The kiln would have been topped with a wattle dome.

Remains of the corn-drying kiln bowl near Kirkmichael

Farm buildings and turf roofs

In medieval times, farming was at a subsistence level, each community aiming to be self-sufficient. The farm might have several buildings and small enclosures or kailyards for vegetables, with arable land and pasture beyond. Houses were sometimes shared for warmth, with people and cattle living at opposite ends of a byre-dwelling.

You will see the ruins of shielings in several places: see the photograph on page 56. A shieling was a small settlement on higher ground where sheep and cattle grazed in the warmer months. All summer, the women and children lived in a shieling-hut, a small stone building, minding the animals and making butter and cheese or spinning wool. The earliest shieling-huts were round or oval, but by the late 18th century they were normally oblong. A good site, with a well-drained, level base and a supply of fresh water nearby, would be used repeatedly.

Turf was used as a building material, for example to make walls built on a stone foundation, or to form a roof resting on timber joists. Peat and wattle were also sometimes used in the past. The excellent insulating quality of turf has made its use survive into the 21st century. The Log Cabin Hotel in Kirkmichael also functions as the headquarters of Norlog, a company which to this day builds log cabins with turf roofs (see www.norlog.co.uk).

Turf roofs sometimes need lawn-mower access

2·3 Munros, Corbetts and Grahams

- A Munro is a Scottish mountain whose summit is over 3000 feet (914 m) in height, provided its peak is adequately separate from any neighbouring Munro. If a climber can quickly and easily reach another summit, the lower of the two will be classified as merely a 'Top'.

- Munros are named after a London-born doctor called Hugh Thomas Munro (1856-1919). His family estate was at Lindertis, near Kirriemuir, and he spent a lot of time walking in the Scottish hills. He was a founder member of the Scottish Mountaineering Club (1889) and served as its President (1894-97).

- In Victorian times, many people believed that there were only about 30 peaks over 3000 feet, but Munro devoted immense energy to identifying as many as possible. His published table (1891) listed 283 such Summits (and 255 Tops). He was still working on a revised table when he died, and there has been protracted debate about the exact list, and the distinction between a Munro and a Top, ever since. Today's generally accepted figure is 284 Munros and 227 Tops (SMC, 1997).

- The first 'Munroist' was the Rev A E Robertson, who completed his final Munro in Glen Coe in 1901. Since then, the popular sport of 'Munro-bagging' has flourished, with hundreds of people becoming Munroists every year.

- Some determined individuals ascend all the Munros in a single expedition lasting several months, whereas others spread the challenge over a lifetime. In summer 2000, Charlie Campbell, a Glasgow postman, set an extraordinary record by completing the round in just 48 days and 12 hours.

- The Trail passes through Spittal of Glenshee, which has some 20 Munros within range. Determined baggers could collect them all in a short stay here. Indeed the *Glenshee information pack* (see page 63) shows routes for collecting up to eight Munros in a single day (given suitable conditions and experience).

- A Corbett is smaller than a Munro: over 2500 feet (762 m) and with a drop of at least 500 feet all round. The front cover shows a shapely Corbett: Ben Gulabin (806 m), at Spittal of Glenshee. Ben Vrackie and Ben Vuirich near Pitlochry can be seen from various high points around the Trail.

- A Graham is defined in metric units: over 610 m (2001 feet), and with a drop of at least 150 metres (492 feet) all round. An outstanding Graham, Mount Blair is visible from much of the Trail and makes a rewarding climb (see page 41).

Mountain Code

Before you go

Learn the use of map and compass.
Know the weather signs and local forecast.
Plan within your capabilities.
Know simple first aid and the symptoms of exposure.
Know the mountain distress signals.

When you go

Never go alone.
Leave written word of your route, and report on your return.
Take windproofs, waterproofs and survival bag.
Take suitable map and compass, torch and food.
Wear suitable boots.
Keep alert all day.

In winter (November to March)

Each person needs an ice-axe and crampons, and to know how to use them.
The group needs climbing rope, and to know how to use it.
Learn to recognise dangerous snow slopes.

If you need to report an accident on the mountains, telephone the police to ask for Mountain Rescue. To report an accident, telephone the Tayside Police HQ on 01382 223 200 (more direct than dialling 999) with the location, number of persons and any injuries. The police will alert Mountain Rescue and/or the Ambulance Service as appropriate.

Brown hare

2·4 Habitats and wildlife

The Cateran Trail runs through three main types of habitat, described below:

• farmland and river valley

• woodland

• heath and moorland.

If you are keen to spot wildlife, carry binoculars and either walk quietly and alone, or seek fellow-walkers who share your interest and are willing to tread softly. Try to set off soon after sunrise, or go for a stroll in the evening. Animals are much more active at these times than in the middle of the day. Since this applies to midges too, protect your skin thoroughly, especially in summer and in still weather. Fortunately, however, midges are not nearly as troublesome here as in the west of Scotland.

Farmland and river valley

The Trail begins with a riverside walk along the Ericht, and runs through the river valleys of Strathardle, Glen Shee and Glen Isla. You are walking through or alongside farmland for most of its length.

Wild primrose

The rivers are especially rich in bird life. Look out for grey heron in the shallows: sometimes they stand tall and motionless, at other times they stalk their prey. In flight, they trail their legs and their huge grey wings beat very slowly. Near rapids you might see a dipper, a small athletic bird which fearlessly plunges into fast-moving water to catch tiny fish and invertebrates.

Farmland supports a range of animals, from brown hare to small rodents such as field voles and mice, and a range of birds. Look out for the orange-billed oystercatcher, its wings making a white-on-black M-shape in flight, and listen for its piercing shrieks. You will also see lapwings, large black-and-white birds with an iridescent sheen and tall crest. Known locally as 'teuchits', their aerobatic flight is wild and wheeling, their wings distinctively rounded.

Lapwing (adult male)

You may well spot Britain's most widespread bird of prey, the kestrel, which feeds on small mammals, mainly voles and mice. It hovers over the fields by sculling its wings, its sharp eyesight detecting tiny movements below. It hunts in a fast dive with its chestnut-coloured wings half-closed. Near a loch, you might even be lucky enough to sight an osprey, taking fish in its talons and carrying it off torpedo-style.

Woodland

The Trail passes through several large wooded areas: Kindrogan Wood, Calamanach Forest, Blackcraig Forest and the woods around Dalnaglar Castle and Broom Hill. These consist mainly of productive conifers, but also host native species such as aspen, birch, hazel, sessile oak, rowan and Scots pine. These woodlands provide food, nesting sites and shelter for wildlife as well as crops of economic value.

Thistle, with bee

Red squirrel in Scots pine

Scotland has 75% of Britain's red squirrel population and the Trail's forests are a good place to see them. Chewed-up cones lying on the ground are a sign that red squirrels may have been feeding there recently. You may even see them dashing across the road, and drivers should be aware of how vulnerable they are. Apart from vehicles, only one predator is agile enough to catch a red squirrel – the pine marten. It became almost extinct in Britain and is a protected species.

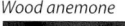

Wood anemone

In spring, the forest floor may be carpeted with bluebells or wood sorrel. Look out also for yellow primrose and celandine, wild violets, and the delicate pale stars of the wood anemone, which flourishes in shady deciduous woodlands.

Red and roe deer are native to Scotland. They are easy to distinguish: roe deer are much smaller than red, they prefer woodland to open spaces, and they appear in small numbers. Their red cousins began in woodland, but under environmental pressure they managed to adapt to living on the uplands and moors. So if you see a distant herd of deer on the skyline, they will be red deer.

Heath and moorland

The Trail's higher ground features open moorland with acid peaty soil and a few trees. Often these are Scots pine, the only pine native to Britain. Heather flourishes in such conditions, and bilberry (blaeberry) sometimes coexists with it. All of the Part 4 walks include sections that are densely carpeted with heather. There are shorter heathery sections on the Trail, for example south of Kirkmichael, approaching the Lairig Gate and on Cairn Hill, south of Kirkton of Glenisla.

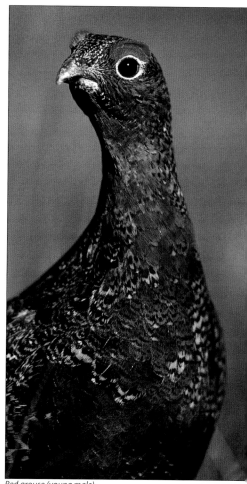

The red grouse is perhaps the iconic bird of the Highland moors. Its colour is closer to rust-brown than red, and it is much commoner than its endangered black cousins, which prefer moorland mixed with woodland. Its loud 'go-back' cackle is unmistakeable, and if you startle one by accident, it will erupt into sudden flight on whirring wings.

Grouse need heather of a suitable range in size and age: they feed on tender young shoots, but need taller plants for ground cover and nesting. On many estates, the heather is managed (burned) for grouse, sometimes leaving large charred areas.

If you see pathways of nibbled heather and blaeberry, look for mountain hare, which turns white in winter. Even in summer, the mountain hare looks different from its brown cousin: its ears are much shorter and its tail lacks the black tip. Hare predators include fox and golden eagle.

Red grouse (young male)

Curlew on its nest, with chick

In summer, you may well hear the burbling, melancholy cry of the curlew, like an old-fashioned kettle approaching the boil. The curlew, Europe's largest wader, breeds and lives on these moorlands in spring and summer, moving to the coast in winter. Its long, curving beak is adapted for feeding on worms and shellfish, and its long legs assist wading through marshes and mud-flats.

Buzzard are also known as 'the tourist's eagle', because visitors so often mistake them for eagle. Golden eagles have a wing-span of two metres, double that of the buzzard, and they range over remote areas: consider yourself very lucky if you see one. Buzzard are much commoner. Recognise them by their soaring flight on air currents, with wings held in a shallow Vee. They call with a distinctive mewing, especially in the breeding season, and sometimes perch on isolated trees or even fence-posts.

Floral display at the Wellmeadow

Joined as a single town by Act of Parliament in 1928, Blairgowrie and Rattray lie on opposite banks of the River Ericht, and the signage of today still retains their separate names. Until 1777 when the Brig o' Blair was built, the two communities were linked only by a coble ferry (a traditional rowing boat).

Blairgowrie, known locally as 'Blair', had been a modest village of 400 folk in the 18th century, but its population increased tenfold during the following century. Its growth was driven by the textile mills which harnessed the river's energy to power spinning machines and looms for flax, and later jute.

Visit the Tourist Information Centre on the Wellmeadow (see page 62) to find out more about the town and its environs.

27

'Berry capital of the world'

In 1898 James Mackenzie Hodge, a solicitor, noticed the quality of the wild raspberries, which flourish in the local climate and soil. He planted several acres, and Blair soon became famous as the 'berry capital of the world'. From all over Scotland, thousands of people gathered to pick the fruit, spending their evenings telling stories and singing traditional songs. Nowadays, many fruit-pickers are students from mainland and eastern Europe.

Hamish Henderson (1919-2002) was born in Blairgowrie and became a leader of the 20th century Scottish folk revival. Like Robert Burns two centuries earlier, he played a major role in preserving the Scots oral tradition. Henderson was inspired by the exuberant songs of the berry-pickers, and he later described the process of song-collecting as 'holding a tin can under the Niagara Falls.'

Henderson was a highly educated soldier, poet and songwriter. His talent for modern languages led to his career in military intelligence during the Second World War in North Africa and Italy. In 1944, he accepted the surrender of Italian forces. Post-war, he campaigned for peace and anti-imperialism. His own legacy of fine ballads includes *The Freedom Come-all-ye* and *Ballad of the D-Day Dodgers*, a biting satire reflecting his wartime experiences in Italy.

Berry-pickers, Blairgowrie, 1950

3·2 Blairgowrie to Kirkmichael

Map	panels 1 and 2
Distance	15 miles (24.5 km)
Terrain	mainly pleasant footpath and open tracks with a few streams to cross; very little road-walking
Grade	some modest ascents and descents, with the number of stiles making for slower progess than you might expect north of Bridge of Cally
Food and drink	Blairgowrie, Bridge of Cally, Kirkmichael
Summary	a varied first day, from the banks of the Ericht via farmland to the splendid moorland path to Bridge of Cally; after Blackcraig forest, enjoy open views over Strathardle and the descent to Kirkmichael

River Ericht

Blairgowrie — 7 — 11 — Bridge of Cally — 8 — 13½ — Kirkmichael

- The Trail begins at the ironwork finger-post on the south side of the bridge over the River Ericht, which points down steps to the riverside walk. Follow the Trail upstream to and through the car park. The riverside path is a prime place to spot dippers darting over the river and catching fish.

- Soon, a flight of timber steps takes you to a higher level, still following the river upstream. There are brief diversions to a salmon observation platform with an interpretation board, and also to Cargill's Leap: see panel.

Cargill's Leap

The minister Donald Cargill (born Rattray 1610) was persecuted by King Charles II's anti-presbyterian government. He escaped pursuing soldiers by leaping the Ericht at this point. Later he was caught, convicted of treason and executed in Edinburgh in 1681.

The Leap no longer looks possible, with good reason: in 1960 the Council widened the channel with explosives, to discourage children from dangerous attempts to copy Cargill's exploit. It is still a dramatic spot, in its gorge of red sandstone conglomerate, some 350 million years old. The strange pot-holes were formed over centuries by the scouring action of water and sand.

- Shortly, you see a footbridge across the River Ericht on your right. Make a small detour for the river view and information board about the mills. You are facing the (disused) grain mill. Most of the Ericht's mills were for jute and flax, and some were later converted for synthetics.

- Here you bear left uphill to a private road which goes past more mills and houses, soon reaching a minor tarmac road.

- Turn left up the minor road which climbs steeply south (back towards Blairgowrie). Within about 500 m, after a fine viewpoint over the river and Rattray, look for the turning up a still narrower road, where you turn right (west).

- Walk up this broken-surfaced road, which climbs steadily, soon veering south-westerly. After 1.5 km, it levels out and turns right (north-west).

- Follow the road to East Gormack, where a succession of wicket-gates lead round the farm, channelling walkers through a narrow path, fenced on both sides.

- Soon the Trail turns left, right, then left again, punctuated by wicket-gates. In places, the path is narrow and fenced on both sides.

- This section finishes with 1 km of path which broadens somewhat, but is still fenced. It ends at the very minor road to Middleton, where you turn right (heading north).

- Walk along this road (a single-track no-through road, so traffic is light) for 1 km until it ends at Middleton Farm.

- Walk straight through the farm buildings and follow the waymarker over the stile and uphill on the farm road. Soon the Trail turns left and passes through a wicket-gate. From here on, beware of cattle (see page 10). Follow the Trail as it forges due north, through another wicket-gate.

- After a pedestrian gate, you reach open moorland, with fine stone walls. Continuing north, you pass birch woodland, hemmed in by more stone walls. After this, you cross sheep moorland punctuated by wicket-gates, and may have your first glimpse of Mount Blair (see photograph on page 33).

- Finally you pass over a stile and descend through mixed woodland on a deeply rutted road; it may be easier to walk along its high grassy verge. Near its end it curves, and after a hairpin left you reach a very minor tarmac road.

- Here the Trail divides: turn left (west) to continue the Trail to Kirkmichael without a pause, or turn right for Bridge of Cally and its Hotel (open daily year-round, walkers welcome).

 To walk the Trail anti-clockwise via Alyth, turn left at the Hotel, cross the bridge and turn right along the A93.

- To resume the Trail clockwise, return to the dividing point, and head westward along the loose-surfaced road, past a sign saying 'Kirkmichael 7.5 miles'.

- Soon the road passes through a metal gate into Blackcraig Forest and starts to climb gently through the conifers. The trees are mainly set well back from the road. Occasional clearings allow open views over the Ardle and its strath (valley), with distant mountains to the north.

- Two km after Bridge of Cally, the forest road swings right (north-west) and starts a gentle descent. Note the splendid ancient drystone walls in this section, supporting a variety of mosses and wild flowers.

- You emerge from the forest at Bothy Cottage, with its pretty garden pond, and turn left (still north-westerly) up a rustic road between a fine avenue of trees. Keep straight on past several more houses.

- Soon bear left uphill and turn left off the road, into a field with ponies. Cross the field uphill, then turn right and descend to pass through or over a gate.

- Here you turn left to pick up a pleasant green road with good views, with a glimpse of the ruins of Blackcraig Castle Tower.

- Passing over a cattle grid, you bear left uphill on a stony path with a small burn on your left and a larch plantation on your right. Soon you bear left uphill and cross the burn by a stone bridge.

- You follow the path uphill, but the Trail immediately bears right to pass over a tall stile. You continue along a narrow path with stone walls and fine open views. After further stiles, high and low, you start a gentle descent.

- The narrow path broadens and passes by stone walls, a plantation and along the top margin of a field. Pass through or over a gate, and negotiate a boggy bit among the rhododendrons.

- Soon you cross Pitcarmick Burn, set in its miniature Himalayan gorge, and follow the wide green path curving right and downhill toward the settlement. Short of these buildings, however, the Trail turns left and left again, uphill steeply to a small stile.

- Turn right to pass along the top of the field (with care, because of boggy ground and an awkward slope) and pass over another tall stile into the heathery moorland. Look out for waymarkers as you cross the heather: the Trail rises above the line of the bottom fence, but its waymarkers are widely spaced here.

- Cross various streams: where there is no footbridge, choose your stepping-stones carefully if the burn is in spate. Finally cross the fence by a stile, then a waymarker sends you left along a forestry road. Look back from here to see Loch Dalvey, which is curiously hard to see until you have passed it.

Pitcarmick Burn

- After a cattle-grid you head north along a rough road, which undulates through a section of forest featuring ladder stiles and old stone walls. After the forest, there are further open views and the long curving descent into Kirkmichael begins, passing through or over various gates.

- You know you are close when you can look up to the left and see the distinctive log cabin buildings of the estate at Balnald, including the Log Cabin Hotel. Just below the Trail to the right, note the fine example of a lime-kiln (see page 17).

- Soon a waymarker takes you right across a timber bridge over the Balnald Burn (a tributary of the Ardle). In under 1 km you arrive in Kirkmichael on a minor road which reaches a T-junction just past the kirk (now part of the riding stables). To reach the Log Cabin Hotel, turn left at the kirk and follow the signs.

- Otherwise, turn right and immediately you face a further T-junction at Kirkmichael Primary School. To continue the Trail, turn left in front of the school. To reach the village shop, Post Office and parish church, turn right and follow the road across the bridge over the Ardle, to the main road (A924).

Looking north from the moorland, towards Mt Blair

3·3 Kirkmichael to Spittal of Glenshee

Map	**panel 2**
Distance	**8 miles (13 km)**
Terrain	**farm road and footpaths followed by forest and grassy road giving way to a rough narrow path; there are some boggy bits and streams to cross**
Grade	**an easy walk to Enochdhu, then a steady but not taxing ascent to the Lairig Gate (650 m/2130 ft), followed by the descent to Spittal which is steepish at first**
Food and drink	**Kirkmichael, Spittal**
Summary	**a fine walk through an unspoiled glen, with glorious views from the Trail's high point where you cross from Strathardle into Glenshee**

Log cabins with turf roofs are a feature of Kirkmichael

- Return to the school to pick up the Trail as it leaves Kirkmichael, rising above the riverside walk signposted off to your left. Enjoy the views over flat fields punctuated by drystone dyke walls, streams and the odd stand of Scots pines. At first you walk on a no-through road, then on a rough farm road.

- Less than 2 km from the village, the road approaches Loch Cottage, but the Trail bears off left on a narrow boggy path around house, garden and loch. The path soon enters the forest where it crosses various streams and has various boggy stretches.

- You emerge from the forest over a stile to enjoy fine open views over Dalreoch (a large white house followed by some B&Bs) and pass a sign to Kindrogan Field Centre.

- Approaching Enochdhu, you cross the River Ardle by Kindrogan Bridge, a historic site (see page 15). Pass the car park, and cross the main road. Before continuing the Trail uphill towards Dirnanean Farm, consider a 100 m diversion to your right along the main road to see Ardle's Grave (see panel).

Ardle's Grave

Although it lies in a private garden, this long burial mound (almost 6 m long by 1 m wide) with its standing stone is clearly visible from the roadside. The Danes invaded the Enochdhu area in around AD 903, but were beaten off by the Picts. Prince Ardle (Ard-fhuil, or 'of noble blood') probably led the Picts, but he was killed in battle and this mound marks his noble grave. It is shown on OS maps as the 'Giant's Grave', but this is misleading: he was of normal stature, but is probably buried with one or two of his henchmen. The river and its entire strath (valley) later became known by Ardle's name.

Loch Cottage

Kirkmichael — 2½ / 4 — Enochdhu — 3 / 5 — Upper Lunch Hut — 2½ / 4 — Spittal of Glenshee

Upper Lunch Hut offers shelter to walkers

- Return to the sign 'Public footpath to Spittal of Glenshee' on your right, and follow the farm road uphill to Dirnanean Farm. It climbs steadily, reaching the Estate Office after 10 minutes and the Home Farm Steading soon after. Here you make a well-signposted left turn as the footpath turns to pass through (or climb over by means of stiles) the timber gates, continuing to gain altitude.

- After another 15 minutes you turn left over a stile into Calamanach Wood (planted 1988). The plantation is set well back from the forestry road, with a few deciduous trees along its margins, and its surface makes for easy, pleasant walking. As you continue to climb steadily, views begin to open up to the west and north.

Standing-stone on Trail above Dirnanean

- At the end of the forest, after another 15 minutes or so, you exit by another gate (Greengate) into open moorland, with nearby hills on both sides, and more distant views to the south-west.

- Heading north-east, the grassy road climbs at first, then dips a little and climbs again with a small waterfall on your right. Cresting the rise, you soon see Upper Lunch Hut on your left, a timber shelter kindly provided by the estate, complete with lunch tables and Visitors' Book. Note the entry concerning Queen Victoria's horseback visit here in 1865.

- Heading on uphill, you cross a burn on stepping stones (care needed if in spate). Immediately afterwards the route veers right (east) and narrows noticeably to a heathery path. After it crosses another, much smaller burn, the gradient increases and you sense that you are leaving this glen for the next. Behind you, if you are lucky, lies a splendid view over the distant mountains of Schiehallion and the Lawers group, snow-covered in winter and spring.

- Approaching the top, the path narrows to a passage between hillsides. Finally, some 45 minutes after Upper Lunch Hut, you reach the summit (650 m), the Lairig Gate. Its sign suggests times – 'Glenshee 20 minutes, Enochdhu 1 hour 20 minutes' – that are over-optimistic even for walkers heading downhill.

- Just beyond this gate, a new vista opens out. Glen Shee runs below you from north-west to south-east, with the A93 road snaking through it. Your destination, the village of Spittal, lies in clear view.

- The Trail descends by a pleasant grassy path through sheep grazing land, soon picking up a stream which joins from the left. You cross the stream further down, and its plashing accompanies you all the way to Spittal, growing in volume as it loses height.

- Reaching the corner of the stone-walled sheep enclosure, cross over a tall stile and, after a short steep slope, cross the stream again. Lower down, it has cut steep sides into the ground, forming rapids and small falls which are impressive when in spate.

- The footpath emerges onto the A93, where you turn left to continue the Trail, or turn right and cross the road to the Spittal of Glenshee Hotel (see pages 16 and 20). Located at a strategic point on the cattle drove routes, it claims to be the oldest operating inn site in Britain, first chronicled in AD 961.

Looking south-west from below the Lairig Gate

3·4 Spittal of Glenshee to Kirkton of Glenisla

Map	panels 2 and 1
Distance	14 miles (22.5 km)
Terrain	the first 5 miles (8 km) is on rough moorland path with boggy bits and several stream crossings, with the remainder on minor roads
Grade	gradients are slight for most of the day, although the off-road section includes some rugged walking
Food and drink	Spittal, Kirkton
Summary	after some rough walking in Glen Shee, the Trail reaches Glen Isla largely by road, with the option to ascend Mount Blair en route; see pages 58-60 for an alternative

Four stones mark the Tomb, see page 39

- To continue with the Trail, follow the minor road through the village, walking across the Old Brig, the bridge built in 1748 as part of the military road from Edinburgh to Fort George.

- Turn left after the bridge to see the slate standing stone which tops an impressive mound of glacial deposit, above you and to your right as you walk briefly upstream between river and Kirk. The graveyard has a number of interesting gravestones.

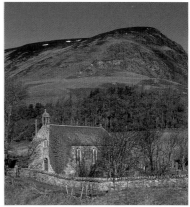
The Kirk at Spittal

- Returning to the road, pass through the village and cross the A93 with care. Go left along the grassy verge for 100 m to the stile, which takes you over the fence of Old Spittal Farm.

- Cross the stream by the timber footbridge, bear left and follow the obvious road uphill and eastward towards the steading. Just after a derelict building, you pass over a stile: within 50 m, look out for some isolated trees above you to the left.

- To divert for the Tomb (see panel), leave the Trail here and walk steeply uphill between the scattered trees towards a patch of scree. Climb past the scree and soon you will see a large mound (see main photograph on pages 8 and 38) with four standing stones. NB: the Tomb is at grid reference 117 701, i.e. 500 m further west than shown on OS Explorer 387.

The Tomb

The Tomb is the legendary and atmospheric sixth century burial place of Diarmid, the great warrior nephew of King Fingal. His love of Fingal's queen Grainne recalls the Arthurian legend in which Launcelot's love of King Arthur's wife Guinevere brings about the fall of Camelot. In an echo of Wagner's Ring Cycle, the jealous fight was resolved in the hunt for a wild boar. Although Diarmid managed to kill the boar in a desperate battle, he was poisoned by its spines. Fingal refused him the antidote, and Diarmid is buried, according to legend, under this mound. Its four stones create the shape of a spearhead which points to where the boar died. Clan Campbell consider themselves to be descendants of Diarmid, and their badge is the head of a wild boar.

- Return to the Trail across the hillside. After passing through or over the next gate, the track approaches the renovated steading, but turns left uphill, in front of it.

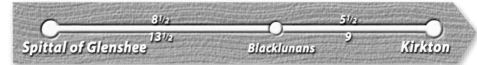

Spittal of Glenshee 8½ 13½ Blacklunans 5½ 9 Kirkton

View from Mount Blair

- Shortly you reach a new deer fence, where you turn right. You will follow this line for several km towards Runavey, where you may wish to make a choice of route.

- The Trail passes an old stone sheep dip, through some seriously boggy bits and descends steeply to cross several streams, with waymarkers scarce. Keep walking south-east below the line of the fence, and you should not have problems.

- Approaching Runavey, the Trail swings eastward, and you may encounter some cattle: see page 10.

- Just after some ruined buildings, the Trail descends to a stile, crosses a stream on a footbridge and after a boggy bit, tapers to a narrow path. This crosses a well-defined and broader 4x4 road. To continue on the Trail, cross straight over the 4x4 road. To follow the off-road alternative to Folda, turn left (see page 58).

- The Trail continues southerly and downhill, passing around the estate of Glenshee Lodge (Compass Christian Centre), fringed by Scots pines. You follow the Trail's circuitous path over several stiles and up a minor road around the private land of a modern house. Turn right opposite its access road, soon passing a stone cross memorial above you and to the left.

- Walk across a field and cross a river by footbridge, climbing the next stone wall by a stile. The Trail swings left then right around the edge of a field, then uphill past birch trees. There is then an awkward stream to cross: choose your crossing-place carefully. Afterwards, follow the line of the fence and wall.

- In the next section, the Trail runs over rough, bouldery, boggy ground above a stone wall, with some impressive crags above you to the left. Then it crosses the wall and picks up easier going on a farm road lower down.

- After passing some farm buildings, you climb over a stile and cross various streams and further stiles, skirting the edge of a forest.

- The Trail goes left uphill over a stile round the corner of the forest, but first it's worth walking a few yards to the right where you will find a fine ford across the Water of Shee. You have now come 5 miles (8 km) from Spittal, and this is a lovely spot to stop for a rest , to paddle in the river or to watch the wildlife. The ford appears still to be passable by some vehicles, and you can see stone pillars – all that survive from a former bridge.

- Once you set off through the forest, you walk uphill past the gardens of Dalnaglar Estate where you will glimpse Dalnaglar Castle and its pond, from a pleasant private road with overhanging trees. Soon the road joins the B951 and the Trail heads straight along it. (To climb Mount Blair, instead turn left along the B951, see panel.)

Mount Blair

Follow the B951 easterly for 1 km as far as a gate on your right leading to the mobile telecom mast at the summit. Climb the gate and follow the rough access road which ascends steadily, sometimes steeply, at first south-easterly. After it veers right, cross a deer fence at the gate and continue to climb steeply. Your effort is soon rewarded by a panoramic view from the summit: on a clear day you can see up to 37 Munros (see page 20), including Ben Nevis, 62 miles away. The low circular shelter features a superb engraved viewfinder showing mountain shapes, altitudes and distances off, commissioned by a local resident. From leaving the Trail, allow at least 2 hours for the round trip (2 km road walk plus 380 m altitude gain).

Cray Parish Church

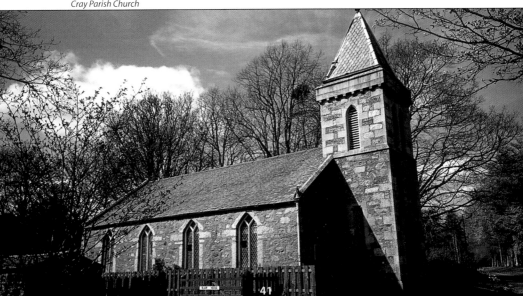

- The Trail sign proclaims 'Spittal 5 miles, Glenisla 8 miles', but don't be discouraged. This understates how far you have come already, and progress is always slower when walking off-road.

- Continue south-west for 700 km until you reach Cray, with its fine old Church, see page 41. Here the B951 continues south-west across the Water of Shee to Lair (see page 52), but the Trail bears left, southward for Blacklunans, along a single-track road with passing places.

- As the road climbs, there are pleasant views to your right over Glen Shee and its river, with some impressive crags lying beyond. Mount Blair lies on your left, and is your companion for over 10 km of road-walking.

- After passing Mountblair Lodge, surrounded by daffodils in spring, you have another 2 km along an undulating fenced road to reach the junction where you turn left, to head easterly. The tiny settlement of Blacklunans has little more than a phone box and pillar-box and a few houses.

- About 1.5 km after Blacklunans you reach Drumore Loch, pleasantly framed by trees and reeds, with a boat-house. The slopes of Nether Craig rise steeply to your left; major efforts were needed to contain its massive boulders. The rocks are rugged and dramatic, even when carpeted with primroses. You may feel a sense of relief once you escape from their potential rockfall.

The rocky slope of Nether Craig rises from the Trail

- Reaching the gentler foothills of Mount Blair, you see heather moorland to your right, rich in curlew, lapwing and grouse. The road descends gently alongside the Alrick Burn, which feeds Brewlands Loch (some 3 km after Drumore Loch), and is surrounded by prime farmland.

- After the loch, you approach Bridge of Brewlands, where the Trail crosses the River Isla by an indirect but well-signposted route. Using the road bridge, it diverts around a farm, turning left, then right along the B951, then right again. (Ignore the obsolete route shown by OS Explorer 387 south of Bridge of Brewlands.)

- Follow the B951 for a further 2.5 km to reach Kirkton of Glenisla. Just after its primary school, notice the Trail signpost off to the right, to which you will return the next day. Continue straight on to reach the village centre and the Glenisla Hotel.

Water of Shee near Blacklunans

3·5 Kirkton of Glenisla to Alyth

Map	**panel 1**
Distance	**11 miles (17.5 km)**
Terrain	**mainly on heathery paths and grassy or loose-surfaced roads, with boggy sections and several stiles, but hardly any tarmac**
Grade	**steady climb out of Kirkton, then slightly undulating route parallel to the River Isla; a short climb to 220 m (720 ft) precedes the steady descent into Alyth**
Food and drink	**Kirkton, Alyth**
Summary	**fine open views over Kirkton of Glenisla lead to an airy walk high above the River Isla, then passing through Kilry Wood; more farmland is followed by the descent between the Hills of Alyth and Loyal into Alyth**

The Trail below Ardormie, with poplars

- Return to the Trail signpost and follow it across the River Isla by the interesting ironwork and timber footbridge. Alyth is a mile further than the signpost claims, and today's walk is mostly off-road.

- After the footbridge, turn left and follow the waymarkers steeply uphill through the heather, around the shoulder of Cairn Hill. On a clear day, the small diversion to its summit (345 m) is well rewarded by the mountain views beyond Kirkton to the north.

- The waymarkers take you south-east and over a stile to a well-defined path. Bear left through the muddy gap in the derelict stone wall to reach a wide path through mixed woodland.

- This section is splendidly airy, with great views over the River Isla and to the north, with springy turf underfoot and bird-song all around. The Trail generally echoes the course of the Isla below, crossing various field boundaries by means of stiles.

- The Trail continues, sometimes on rough track, sometimes on farm road, past Cammock Lodge, across Cammock Burn and through Cammock Farm. Passing between Easter Cammock Farmhouse and a shed, you soon emerge on a sandy-surfaced road.

- Follow the road through the entrance gate to Kilry Woodland Estate (with cattle grid) and hairpins uphill. Turn right uphill along the tarmac road and continue through the forest, with glimpses across Glen Isla to the whaleback of Craiglea Hill.

- Pass through the farm, and turn left after passing several houses. After Drumgell and Westwood, you reach a minor road. Turn right to follow this road very briefly.

The Old Schoolhouse

- Within 100 m, turn left at the Old Schoolhouse. The signpost 'Glen Isla 4, Alyth 6' understates both distances slightly. The road climbs for 500 m, then turns left and descends.

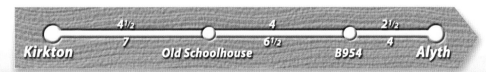

Kirkton — 4½ / 7 — Old Schoolhouse — 4 / 6½ — B954 — 2½ / 4 — Alyth

- Within 500 m, the Trail turns sharp right to leave the road, climbing briefly before turning left to level out and resume its south-easterly trend. The Trail crosses successive fields and streams by footbridge, planks and many stiles. However, at all points it is clearly marked.

- The Trail follows a boggy, sunken ditch with a small patch of birch woodland above it on the right. If it seems impossibly wet, use the woodland for a while.

- After the Trail rises out of its ditch, it follows the fence along the bottom of the field, with open views to the left. It turns right (southerly) and climbs stiffly uphill, flanked by mature sycamore trees.

- After undulating across a couple of fields, the Trail bears right (south-west) and you pass through a prickly gorse-filled passage bounded by fence. Finally you emerge to turn left down the farm road towards Ardormie, then left again along the minor road.

- The road from Ardormie leads gently downhill past a fine row of poplars, to meet another minor road. Here you bear right, then right again, due south along the B954. The signpost shows Alyth as 4 miles by road, but the Trail takes half that distance.

- After 250 m of road walk, keep straight on (still southerly) for about 3 km on the path to Alyth, signposted as the Hill of Loyal Walk.

- After the wicket-gate, you follow an undulating line of trees with sheep grazing peacefully in the fields beside.

- After another wicket-gate, cross a stream and follow the tree-lined path southwards, passing between the Hill of Alyth on your right and the Hill of Loyal to your left.

Hill of Alyth (295m)

The Hill of Alyth is Mount Blair in miniature. It stands in isolation, and the rewards of the view from its summit is out of all proportion to the effort involved in reaching it. Simplest is to follow the Trail southward to the wicket-gate at 249 499, then double-back north-west for the 700 or so metres to the summit, returning by the same route. It might seem tempting to try a cross-country route, but it is not advised. Using the track, the round trip takes less than an hour, including time to enjoy the view.

- After a gentle descent, you reach another wicket-gate. Leave the Trail here to ascend the Hill of Alyth (see panel).

 If walking the Trail anti-clockwise, at this wicket-gate keep due north along the line of the fence: do not be misled into bearing left up the Hill of Alyth.

- Exit by the wicket-gate and descend the rough road past the reservoir and hotel – the Loyal Road into Alyth.

- At its foot, turn right into Hill Street. For the town centre and its amenities, turn left, leading to Commercial Street. To continue the Trail, keep straight along Hill Street, which becomes High Street, soon to bear right up Bamff Wynd.

Alyth is a small town full of history, for centuries a market centre dealing in cattle droving and the wool, jute and linen trades. At its centre is the Market Square, with an Old Market Cross dating from 1670, but relocated here in 1913. Alyth Burn runs through the town, which features many footbridges including the 16th century packhorse bridge. Alyth Museum is worth a visit, see page 62 for opening times.

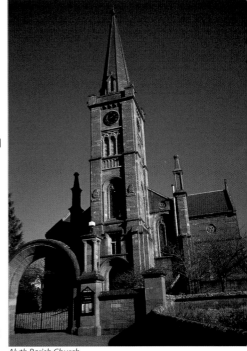

Alyth Parish Church

Alyth has had a Christian presence since the 6th century, when St Moluag (a contemporary of St Columba) founded its original Old Church. The famous Alyth Arches (see photograph on page 48) still stand on the site of the former church. Alyth Parish Church, completed in 1839 to Thomas Hamilton's design, commands the upper town with its unusually tall spire and warm red sandstone. There is a tall Pictish cross-slab in its porch, and the church may be open to visitors in July/ August (Saturdays 10-12 am and Sundays 2-4 pm).

The Loyal Road descending into Alyth

3·6 Alyth to Blairgowrie

Map	**panel 1**
Distance	**16 miles (26 km)**
Terrain	**moorland paths and estate roads give way to a stretch of tarmac, followed by rough road and path, with minor road into Bridge of Cally; finally footpaths and tracks lead back to Blairgowrie**
Grade	**gradients are modest; the Trail twice climbs over 290 m/950 ft en route for Bridge of Cally**
Food and drink	**Alyth, Bridge of Cally, Blairgowrie**
Summary	**leaving Alyth, the Trail passes over moorland and skirts around the Bamff Estate then to follow 4 km of minor road; after an off-road section, it descends to Bridge of Cally, then returns via moorland and farmland to Blairgowrie**

Footbridges over Alyth Burn, with Alyth Arches at upper centre

- The Trail heads north-west out of Alyth. From the High Street at the top of the town, turn right up Bamff Wynd. Keep right past West Quarter Farm, and follow its farm road steadily uphill. (The sign saying 'Bridge of Cally 10' here overstates the mileage.)

- Follow the road as it curves left after 1 km, but immediately turn right into a narrower path, making a dog-leg, and continuing to climb northerly. The Hill of Alyth is prominent ahead to your right, and wide views are opening out on your left. Behind you to the south is a panorama over Alyth.

- Soon you pass through a wicket-gate into open hillside and approach a lochan (small loch) on your right. Watch carefully for waymarkers showing where the Trail veers left (westerly), across the gorse and heather. There are fine views to the north, and you may glimpse Backwater Reservoir.

 NB If doing Trail anti-clockwise, look out for the easily missed waymarker directing you to bear right (south) before you pass this lochan.

- You pass another, much smaller lochan on your left and cross two larger grassy roads, to descend down a narrow path. Waymarkers are sparse here, so look out for them carefully. After a wicket-gate, you reach a minor road, which you cross diagonally to the right. (Ignore the OS Explorer 381 which here shows the Trail turning left along the road.)

- Follow the waymarkers to continue northerly down the farm track and over a stile into the Bamff estate. Walk up the farm road between hedgerows, opening into a wider road framed by spreading beech trees. Don't be too worried by the notice 'Wild boar, keep out' as boars tend to be shy, except during the mating season (autumn).

- The Trail turns left among the rhododendrons and pursues a shady path with a mixture of stately trees and shrubs. Just after you pass around the massive fallen tree, you turn right along the private road that approaches Bamff Lodge.

Alyth — 9 / 15 — Bridge of Cally — 7 / 11 — Blairgowrie

- Bear right at the fork near the house, towards the Old Dairy. Look for a discreet waymarker that guides you left in front of the red house. Follow the road as it threads its way amongst the buildings and past scrap cars. The Trail then skirts around three sides of a field and finally descends through woodland to the minor road.

- Turn right at the road, then after 100 m turn left towards the Mains of Creuchies. The sign here says 'Alyth 3, Bridge of Cally 6'.

- Follow the single-track tarmac road for over 4 km: first it descends steeply to the Burn of Alyth and rises more gently on the far side, then it passes through a gateway and enters a pleasant open section between cattle grids, where you can choose your line more freely.

- After Burnside Cottage, you finally escape the tarmac: keeping straight on, you follow first a rough farm road, then a path between fields, with wicket gates and boggy bits. Climbing steadily (to 290 m) you may notice new hedgerows on your right, fine old beeches to the left and open views on both sides.

- The Trail starts to broaden, then it descends, curving left. You will glimpse Bridge of Cally, now only 3 km away. After passing through a number of gates, it emerges as a loose-surfaced road that twists and turns down past Netherton Kirk and across the Black Water by a bridge.

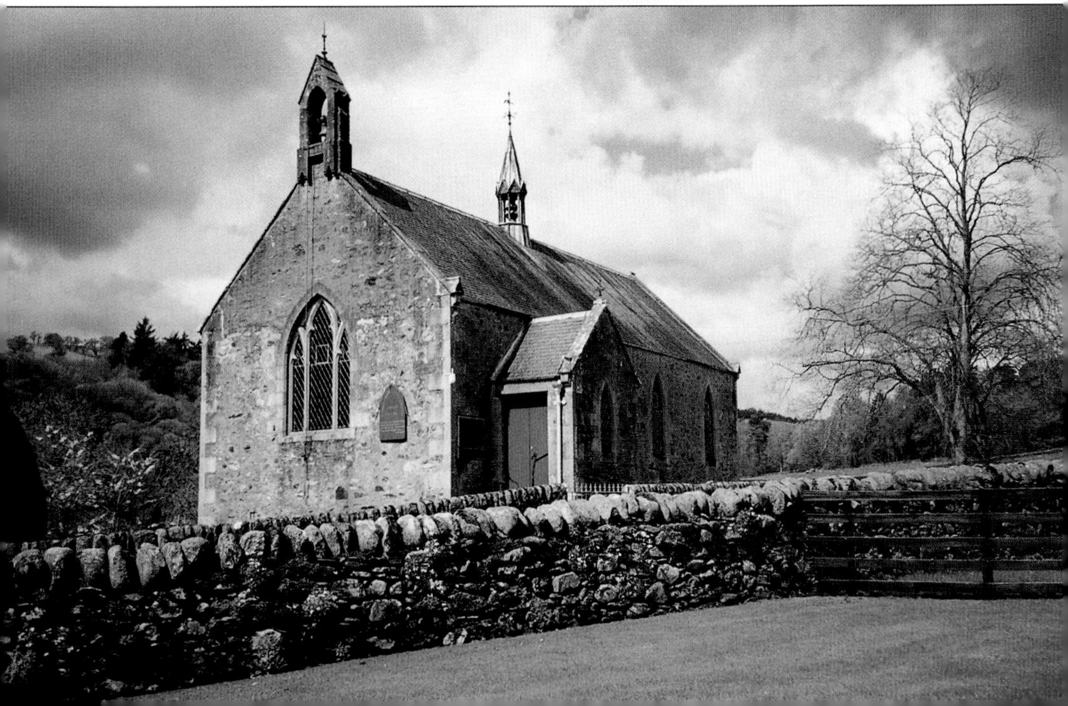

Netherton Kirk

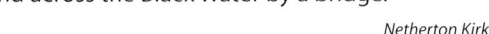

- The minor road then climbs to meet the main A93 where you turn left to enter Bridge of Cally past the school and Post Office. At first, the pavement is incomplete: take great care to see, and be seen by, vehicles on the blind corner. Just after the main bridge over the Ericht, you reach the walker-friendly Bridge of Cally Hotel.

Bridge of Cally Hotel

- To continue the Trail back to Blairgowrie, continue past the back of the Hotel to the waymarker where the Trail splits (see page 31, fifth bullet).

- Turn left (southward) for Blairgowrie, referring to pages 30-31 for a reminder of the outward journey if need be. As you complete your Trail, reflect on how the gentle pace of the modern walker contrasts with the desperate raids of the caterans long ago.

Birch moorland south of Bridge of Cally

4·1 The Cateran Minitrail: Lair to Kirkmichael

The Minitrail is suggested as a weekend experience: see page 7. For simplicity, it is described as running clockwise from Kirkmichael. Follow pages 34-37 (day one) and pages 38-42 as far as Cray (day two). To complete day two, returning to Kirkmichael via Lair off-road, follow the instructions below. The entire Minitrail is about 20 miles (32 km), of which 18 miles is off-road. The section below is about 5 miles (8 km).

Spittal

Lair

Kirkmichael

Note: the suggested route from Lair to Kirkmichael follows a waymarked Right of Way. Although at first the track is not obvious, it follows the hillside contours, and in reasonable conditions it is neither strenuous nor difficult to follow. However, you should carry, and know how to use, a compass as well as a recommended map.

Recommended map: OS Landranger 43 (or Explorer 387), see page 63.

Lair to Kirkmichael

- At Cray's fine church, instead of bearing left for Blacklunans, continue on the B951 and cross the Water of Shee. Within 500 m, you meet the A93 at Lair, where you briefly turn left and cross the busy road with care.

- At the end of the crash barrier, look for the finger-post 'Public footpath to Kirkmichael' marking the stile on the right. Climb the stile, then follow the route as pointed by timber marker posts uphill (westerly), with a burn on your right. After the first short climb the path becomes a bit more obvious. Soon the view opens up to a distant ridge in the north (Creag Leacach).

The sign marking the stile at Lair

- The route, which can be boggy underfoot, veers south-west on a slight rise towards a ladder stile over a boundary dyke. You are now in the watershed between two hills (Creag an Lair and Lamh Dearg). There are yellow-topped marker posts and a rustic finger-post indicating routes to Kirkmichael, Lair and Kilrie.

- Soon, after you cross the hollow and climb to a rocky outcrop, a fine view emerges down the line of the Ennoch Burn to Glenkilrie Wood. You can also see round the shoulder of Lamh Dearg all the way to Ben Gulabin, at Spittal. Hut circles are marked here on some OS maps, and if you look among the boulders you will see the ruins of four or five buildings, marking an old township.

- The path again becomes clearer once it starts to descend to a ladder stile over the boundary dyke, then to a footbridge over the Ennoch Burn.

- After crossing the burn you pursue a 4x4 track across the grouse moor, heading for Ashintully Castle and following waymarkers. After the ladder stile at a fence just beyond a lochan, you leave rough walking and enter the well-maintained pastures around Ashintully (see panel).

i **Ashintully Castle**

Ashintully Castle (not open to the public) was built by Colonel David Spalding in 1583 using the spoils of 7 successful years fighting as a mercenary in Flanders for the King of Spain. The Spaldings were for a time a leading family in Strathardle, and a combative lot, constantly at war with nearly everyone. However, it was a Spalding who established the first cattle market in Kirkmichael, at Sillerburn (see page 14).

- Once across the stile, keep to the left margin of the field to find the next stile. Note the superb quality of the drystone dyke here, with its enormous base stones.

- The Right of Way crosses successive fields which skirt the castle, and leaves through a small stand of larch. Note the *lunkie hole* in the dyke close to the stile at the edge of this wood. Before it became blocked, it would have allowed sheep (but not cattle) to be passed from one field to another.

- Once across this stile, keep to the right around the field margin. The next stile and footbridge are visible at the other end of the field. Once across the Allt Menach burn, the path passes the remains of a larger old settlement, this time of eight or nine houses.

- The view of the strath to the south opens up past Milton Knowe. Head west to the stile in the shadow of a stand of conifers to the left. From there, bear slightly right of the stand of Scots pine on the ridge to pick up the next marker: the track is not well-defined.

- From this marker, or better still from the edge of the rocky outcrop surmounted by pines, you will have the widest view over Strathardle. Ben Vrackie is clearly visible beyond Kindrogan Hill. From here it is downhill all the way to the Kirkmichael Hotel, which has a good selection of cask and bottle ales.

- Below this outcrop lie the ruins of another small farmstead. Among these you will find the remains of a small corn-drying kiln. You can see the semi-circular stone-lined kiln bowl set into the hillside, and the outline of the fire-box that would have been fuelled with peat: see page 18.

- To resume the path, head west from the corn-kiln until you are in line with the last waymarker. The path crosses some boggy ground and is unclear, but the next ladder stile is obvious enough.

- Cross the field to the gate, using the stile if need be. The Right of Way runs along the left of the burn, following a sunken road all the way to the Kirkmichael Hotel.

Rocky outcrop surmounted by Scots pines

4·2 A link with the Rob Roy Way

The Rob Roy Way is a splendid week's walk from Drymen to Pitlochry, following in the footsteps of Scotland's most famous outlaw: see the back cover flap for details of the parallel guidebook. Ambitious long-distance walkers may wish to combine it with the Cateran Trail, making a grand two-week expedition through the Highlands. This section explains how to reach Kirkmichael off-road from Pitlochry or Ballinluig.

Kirkmichael

Pitlochry

Ballinluig

> This route is suitable for those who can use map and compass confidently, relying on good visibility. It passes over exposed treeless moorland, and contains two short sections where there is no clear path. Ballinluig to Kirkmichael is about 14 km by this route: allow 3-5 hours.

Recommended map:
OS Landranger 52 or 53 (but not Explorer 387: see page 63).

- From Pitlochry, first choose how to reach Ballinluig: if walking 10 km along minor roads has little appeal, consider taking a bus. Faster services take 7-10 minutes, but they are not frequent, and times differ at week-ends. Check ahead of time (see page 62), or consider a taxi.

- From Ballinluig, head north-east then east up the minor road signposted for Tulliemet, to reach the entrance to Tulliemet House. Walk up its long drive, noting the impressive tall trees including two magnificent 'monkey puzzles'.

- After nearly 2 km, on its final approach to Tulliemet House, the driveway divides: fork right towards the cottages of the steading. There you will find a farm road amongst the buildings. Turn left up this and follow it uphill, north-easterly.

Above Tulliemet, looking downhill towards Ballinluig

Ruins of a small shieling

- Shortly you pass through a gate into the hillside sheep pasture, then a second gate. The road climbs for a while, then descends to a stream which you cross on stepping-stones (with care).

- Just after the stream, you reach a third gate with sheep pens to its left and farm equipment and a container to its right. Pass through the wicket-gate heading north, but leave the road almost immediately. The easiest way to find the exact point is to count your strides.

- About 45 strides after the gate, cross a timber footbridge. A further 50 strides after that would take you to a much smaller foot-plank. Instead, bear off right about 20 strides *before* the foot-plank. The path is not obvious at first, but head north-east. After 120 strides you should see the remains of a stone structure, probably a small shieling: see its photograph above.

- Leaving the ruins on your right, continue north-east a further 30 strides and the path will become obvious. Head straight for the distinctive whale-back of Sgorr Gorm. Although not labelled on OS Landrangers, its summit is shown as 502 m at grid reference 028 579. You will pass just to the right of this hill: see the photograph on page 57.

- If you can't find the shieling, return to the main track and continue north for another 90 strides beyond the foot-plank. At this point, the right turn towards the faint path is more obvious.

- Within five minutes, the path has become clear and it remains well-defined for the next 5 km. It takes you north-east, directly past Sgorr Gorm, climbing to 455 m at the pass, with impressive crags on your right. On a fine day, it's worth first diverting north over the heather to enjoy the view from Sgorr Gorm's summit.

- Just beyond the highest point, pause to identify your next destination, 2 km away: the corner of the forest at 048 592. This is your goal, since the only footbridge over the Back Burn (or Balnald Burn) is nearby.

- Although the track descends towards your goal at first, after a while it veers too far left: take the first chance to turn right and continue until you escape the heather soon afterwards. Now simply head north-east across the open hillside, aiming at the corner of the forest, and picking the best line to avoid the boggy bits.

- Cross the burn by the footbridge and make a choice: either ascend north-west steeply along the edge of the forest to enter it over the gate at 046 595, following the track as it undulates eastward through the forest, leaving it at 054 595. Alternatively, follow the edge of the forest mainly easterly, then northerly, between fence and fast-flowing burn. This involves some awkward footwork in the narrow sections, and you end by climbing along the forest edge to pick up the track where it leaves the forest at 054 595.

- From here, the clear track continues eastward for 2 km and no further navigational effort is needed. You may feel as if you have arrived in Narnia, as you pass charming turf-roofed log cabins with fairy lights and ornaments. Shortly you reach the Log Cabin Hotel, from where Kirkmichael is just over 1 km downhill.

Looking north-east towards Sgorr Gorm: the arrow points to the pass

4·3 Spittal to Folda via Glen Beanie

This route provides an alternative to walking the Trail as described on pages 40-43, offering more of a wilderness experience. Spittal to Kirkton is about 18 km by this method, saving over 4 km of road-walking.

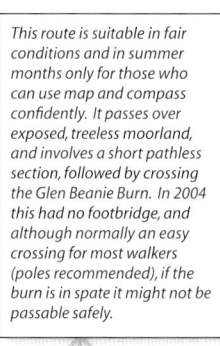

Spittal

Kirkton

Recommended map: OS Landranger 43 (or Explorer 387), see page 63.

- Keep to the Trail past the buildings of Runavey (see page 40). Just after crossing a stream on a footbridge, the Trail tapers to a narrow path which crosses a well-defined and broader 4x4 road (at grid reference 134 689). Here you turn left off the Trail and walk uphill (north-east).

- You enter Invercauld Estate through a well-marked gate, and follow the clear track uphill at first north-easterly, then easterly.

- About 1 km after you left the Trail, the track divides and you must bear right at this fork (143 692). There may be a folded-up estate information board explaining that continuing north-east takes you into stalking territory, and recommending you to bear right for Loch Beanie.

> *This route is suitable in fair conditions and in summer months only for those who can use map and compass confidently. It passes over exposed, treeless moorland, and involves a short pathless section, followed by crossing the Glen Beanie Burn. In 2004 this had no footbridge, and although normally an easy crossing for most walkers (poles recommended), if the burn is in spate it might not be passable safely.*

- The path meanders pleasantly, veering south-easterly and giving fine open views over the heather moors towards Loch Beanie. After over 1 km, you descend to a footbridge over which you cross the Allt Mor burn.

The moorland track above Runavey

- Continue heading easterly for Loch Beanie, climbing the gate over the fence if it is padlocked. The path bears left towards the southern shore, which has a boat house – the first shelter you encounter after leaving the Trail.

- The eastern end of Loch Beanie has a pleasant, sandy beach, but there is no path for over 1 km from here, so you must follow your compass and watch the lie of the land. Start by heading east-south-east for the obvious col, or pass, at 168 683.

- At first there is a helpful fence running just south of easterly, and you can follow its line, keeping well to its left to avoid the very boggy bits. Soon you must cross another fence at right angles to your line of travel, choosing a suitable spot.

- Soon after the col, at around 171 682, cross the Glen Beanie Burn, if it is safe to do so, making use of suitable stepping stones. Keep heading south-east with the burn flowing down on your right, until you pick up a grassy track at around 173 678.

- Follow the track for the next 3 km as it descends south-east, abruptly becoming a broad 4x4 road with a loose surface.

Eastern end of Loch Beanie

Forter Castle

- Pass through the metal gate at the end of the forested area. The track now veers left, but instead you go over the stile or through the tall gate facing you. Descend the delightful twisting path among birch trees and boulders.

- Turn left at the bottom of the path on to a private road serving some cottages. Very soon you reach Dalvanie Cottage, where you turn right along the minor public road.

- Follow the road for 1 km until it forks. Bear left and cross the River Isla by the Bridge of Forter. Over to your right you will see the fine building of Forter Castle: see panel.

- Continue along this road for a further 3.5 km until you rejoin the Trail at Bridge of Brewlands. Complete the walk to Kirkton of Glenisla as on page 43.

Forter Castle

Built in 1560 by the Ogilvy family, this castle was destroyed (along with the Ogilvys' other home at Airlie Castle, near Alyth) in a violent raid by the Campbells in 1640. This act of revenge followed the death in a fight of four Campbells, and was instructed by the Duke of Argyll. The castle stood in ruins for the next 350 years, but its fortune changed in 1988 when it was bought and sensitively restored using traditional materials. It now offers self-catering accommodation (at a price), with a small chapel for weddings and christenings.
www.scottishcastles.co.uk/forter/

5 Reference

Perth & Kinross Countryside Trust

The Cateran Trail is managed and maintained by Perth & Kinross Countryside Trust. The Trust is a partnership between Perth & Kinross Council, Scottish Natural Heritage, Scottish Enterprise Tayside, Forestry Commission Scotland, Perthshire Tourist Board and Gannochy Trust.

The Trust aims to provide and promote opportunities for access and recreation throughout Perth and Kinross, working with local communities, individuals, farmers and landowners. Recent projects have included path improvements and the development of a network of strategic routes for walkers, cyclists and horse-riders. It relies on funding from the public and private sectors and welcomes contributions to support its work.

For more about the work of the Trust, see www.pkct.org. Comments and feedback on the Cateran Trail are always welcome:

tel   +44/0 1738 475255 (fax 475310)

email   **countryside@pkct.org**

The Scottish Outdoor Access Code

The Land Reform (Scotland) Act 2003 recognised access rights over most land and inland water in Scotland, provided that the access is exercised responsibly. It resolved a long-standing debate about whether walkers in Scotland already enjoyed 'freedom-to-roam'. Its emphasis is firmly on the *responsible* exercise of that freedom.

The Act was passed in 2003, but would not become effective for some months after the Scottish Parliament approved the revised Scottish Outdoor Access Code in July 2004. This document spells out detailed rights and responsibilities for both land users and for land managers. It was revised after extensive consultation.

The Code spells out practical examples of how to balance the land user's rights against those of the land manager. For example, access rights do not apply on land on which crops are growing, although managers are encouraged to leave a margin around the edge for access. Access rights do not cover any criminal activity, such as allowing dogs to worry livestock, dropping litter, lighting open fires without permission, poaching, disturbing wild birds, animals and plants, or polluting water. Walkers should continue to follow the Country Code (page 10) and act with common sense and consideration.

In the longer term, the Code may call into question aspects of footpath management that have long been accepted. For an updated summary of the position, consult the Scottish Natural Heritage website at **www.snh.org.uk**. Email SNH at **enquiries@snh.gov.uk**. Its HQ is in Edinburgh, but due to relocate in Inverness.

Contact details

Travel and public transport

Note that most numbers beginning with 0870 cannot be dialled from outside the UK.

For information on public transport, check the Traveline website **www.traveline.org.uk** or phone 0870 608 2 608. It provides details on Strathtay Buses' frequent service between Perth and Blairgowrie, Scottish Citylink's services Edinburgh/Perth and Glasgow/Perth and various services between Pitlochry and Ballinluig. It also carries details of Scotrail and National Rail services to Perth, the nearest railhead: see also **www.nationalrail.co.uk** and **www.scotrail.co.uk**.

A postbus service operates two limited services between Blairgowrie and Spittal of Glenshee (no. 216); and Blairgowrie to Glenisla (via Alyth, no. 215): see **www.postbus.royalmail.com** or phone +44/0 1250 872 766 (before 1pm). The Perth & Kinross Council booklet *Public Transport Guide: Blairgowrie Area* and a map are available from Blairgowrie TIC (see below).

Many airlines operate flights to Edinburgh Airport (which is closer to Perth than Glasgow Airport) from the rest of the UK, from Ireland and from continental Europe. Try the following for budget fares (subject to conditions and availability):

British Airways **www.ba.com**   0870 850 9 850
bmi   **www.flybmi.com**   0870 6070 555
easyJet   **www.easyjet.com** 0870 6000 000
For Edinburgh/Dublin, consider also
Ryanair (**www.ryanair.com)** and Aer Lingus
(**www.aerlingus.com).**

Visitor information

Blairgowrie's Tourist Information Centre offers a free information pack with accommodation addresses for Trail walkers. It is also a source of useful background on the whole area, and is open daily year-round, except in winter when it is closed on Sundays and opening hours are restricted. Contact the TIC by email
blairgowrietic@perthshire.co.uk
phone +44/0 1250 872 960 or post:
Blairgowrie TIC
26 Wellmeadow
Blairgowrie, PH10 6AS

The Perthshire Tourist Board's website is up-to-date and comprehensive for the Perthshire area: **www.perthshire.co.uk**. Other useful websites include **www.walkingwild.com** and **www.ramblers.org.uk/scotland**.

Alyth Museum

This local museum in Commercial Street, Alyth opens in May-September on Wednesday to Sunday afternoons (1pm-5pm). It houses domestic and agricultural items, giving an insight into local history illustrated by photographs. Admission free, enquiries to +44/0 1738 632 488

Accommodation service with baggage transfer

Easyways
Rm 32 Haypark Business Centre
Marchmont Avenue
Polmont
FK2 0NZ
tel: +44/0 1324 714 132
            www.easyways.com
            info@easyways.com

Hostels

The Independent Backpackers Hostels Scotland website is at **www.hostel-scotland.co.uk.** It lists: Gulabin Lodge at Spittal of Glenshee Backpackers Hostel in Atholl Road, Pitlochry Wester Caputh Independent Hostel near Dunkeld.

The Scottish Youth Hostels Association also lists a hostel in Pitlochry, in Knockard Road, Pitlochry, see
            www.syha.org.uk

Camping and caravanning

The following campsites are close to the Trail
Alyth: Five Roads Caravan Park   01828 632255
            www.fiveroadscaravanpark.co.uk
Alyth: Nether Craig Caravan Park 01575 560204
            www.nethercraigcaravanpark.co.uk
Ballintuim Caravan Park   01250 886276
            www.caravan-sitefinder.co.uk
Blairgowrie Caravan Park   01250 872941
            www.holiday-parks.co.uk
Bridge of Cally: Corriefodly Holiday Park
                                    01250 886236
            www.holiday-parks.co.uk

Further reading

The Cairngorms Adam Watson (Scottish Mountaineering Club District Guide, 1992, 6th edition) 0-907521-39-8

Aimed mainly at climbers, this classic SMC publication is good on geology and landforms, especially of the mountains around Glenshee. Expensive, but well worth borrowing, especially if you plan some Munro-bagging from Spittal.

Navigation for Walkers Julian Tippett (Cordee 2001) 1-871890-54-3

Unusually well illustrated with selected map clips and corresponding photographs. Although aimed at beginners, more experienced walkers could benefit from its sound advice.

Glenshee information pack (from the Spittal of Glenshee Hotel at £1.50 a set): 13 A4 pages plus sketch map covering local history/legend, and a dozen graded walks in the area including the Spittal to Folda route (see 4.3), and various suggestions for accessible Munros. Contact the hotel: email **spittalglenshee@aol.com** or tel +44/0 1250 885 215 (fax 885 223).

Recommended maps

Nicolson published a map in 2000 showing the Trail (as it then ran) on a single sheet at 1:50,000. It pre-dates important changes to the route listed below, and is also superseded west of Alyth. This map could be suitable for following the Minitrail (4.1), but not for the walks in either 4.2 or 4.3.

Ordnance Survey marks the Trail on its Explorer maps 381 and 387, which are at 1:25,000, but difficult to use out-of-doors, especially in any wind. The 2001 editions pre-date route changes approaching Kirkton of Glenisla (see p43); also south of Kirkton (p45, second bullet); and north-west of Alyth (p49, middle).

Sheets 53 and 43 of the OS Landranger series (1:50,000) almost cover the Trail area between them, but do not show its route. Either OS series is suitable for 4.1 or 4.3, but Explorer 387 is very misleading for 4.2, showing some tracks that do not exist, and failing to show others that do.

Grid references

In places, we show standard 6-digit grid references (easting, then northing): their use is explained and supported on all OS maps.

Notes for novices

For those who are new to long-distance walking, our website offers suggestions on choosing and using gear, including boots, rucksack, gaiters, poles, water carrier and blister treatment. You will find them at **www.rucsacs.com**. If for any reason you cannot access the website, post a suitably stamped self-addressed to the address on the back of this book.

Weather forecast

The BBC's five-day weather forecast is available from **www.bbc.co.uk/weather/** – simply enter Blairgowrie. Weather information is also on BBC Ceefax page 401 and ITV Teletext page 152.

Acknowledgements

The author wishes to thank Bob Powell (for the idea of the diagram on p18); Alastair Lavery (for advice on Ardle's Grave); and Pete Cooper of the Spittal of Glenshee Hotel (for his local knowledge, directions to the Tomb and the loan of his charming dogs). The publisher is very grateful to Felicity Martin and Sir Robert Megarry for proof-reading.

Above all, the publisher wishes to thank the Perth & Kinross Countryside Trust for its assistance in the production of this guidebook. However, the Trust is not responsible for any errors of fact or expressions of opinion in this book, and any comments on the book should be directed to the publisher, preferably by email to **info@rucsacs.com**.

Photo credits

Peter Jackson p32; **Louis Flood Collection**, Perth Museum & Art Gallery, Perth & Kinross Council p28 (lower); **Jacquetta Megarry** front cover, title page, p5, p6, p8 (both), p9, p10, p11, p14, p15, p16, p17, p19, p21, p22 (lower), p23 (lower), p24 (lower), p25 (upper), p27, p28 (upper), p29, p33, p34, p35, p36 (both), p37, p38, p39, p40, p41, p42 (both), p43, p44, p45, p47 (both), p49, p50, p51 (both), p52, p55, p56, p57, p58, p59, p60, back cover; **Jenny Blair Oliphant** p4; **D M Phillips** of Blairgowrie p48; and the RSPB **www.rspb-images.com** for 5 images: Bob Glover p22 (upper); Andy Hay p23 (upper); Niall Benvie p24 (upper); David Norton p25 (lower); Mark Hamblin p26; anon. p18, p54.

Index